Tina Sederholm is an award-winni
who has journeyed along that l
international event rider to perfor
coming, least of all her. From a con
to follow the rules and her dream
she has turned into an acerbic, big-hearted sweary, insatiably
curious woman who uses poetry to pry open paradoxes such as
the positives of failure, the richness in debt and the quixotic nature
of love.

A multiple slam winner, she has performed at festivals and gigs all over the country for the last fifteen years, including the Royal Albert Hall and the Edinburgh Fringe, where her three solo shows have been awarded four and five star reviews. This is her third collection.

Everything Wrong With You is Beautiful

Tina Sederholm

Burning Eye

BurningEyeBooks
Never Knowingly
Mainstream

Copyright © 2017 Tina Sederholm

The author asserts the moral right under the Copyright, Designs and Patents Act 1988 to be identified as the author of this work.

All rights reserved. No part of this publication may be reproduced, stored in a retrieval system, or transmitted, in any form or by any means without the prior written consent of the author, nor be otherwise circulated in any form of binding or cover other than that in which it is published and without a similar condition being imposed on the subsequent purchaser.

This edition published by Burning Eye Books 2017

www.burningeye.co.uk
@burningeyebooks

Burning Eye Books
15 West Hill, Portishead, BS20 6LG

ISBN 978-1-911570-01-1

For all the beautiful Rowdy prisoners

CONTENTS

CLUES
PREDICTION — 10
THE CASE AGAINST ACROBATICS — 12
THERE WAS THIS GIRL AT THE CRICKET
WHO — 14
CHRISTMAS DAY: A MIRACLE — 15

LOVE AND OTHER MISUNDERSTANDINGS
CONFESSION — 18
MOST OF OUR HISTORY WE FORGET — 19
LOVE STORY — 20
AGAINST LOVE — 21
ALPHA BITCH — 23
HISTORY — 25
IN THE STYLE OF JOHN OSBORNE — 26
ON MARRIAGE — 28

RELUCTANT FEMINIST
WALKING TO WORK — 32
REDRESS — 33
DREAM DATE — 34
THE BECHDEL TEST — 36
LETTER TO MY HEADMISTRESS — 38

THE SLIP
CONSIDER THE CUPCAKE	42
REASONS TO BE GOOD	44
CARCASSONNE	46
LOST THINGS	47
COLD CALL	48
DRONE	50
FAILURE, YOU MAKE ME INTERESTING	51

BROUGHT TO MY KNEES
BECAUSE I LOVE ANIMALS, DON'T I	54
NOBODY SAID	55
NOT YET	56
EVACUATION	57
FUTURE PLANS	58
SIREN	59

TODAY
TWO DRESSES	62
I WILL NOT MAKE GREAT ART TODAY	64
THERE'S NO MONEY IN POETRY, BUT THEN THERE'S NO POETRY IN MONEY EITHER	66
LET YOUR DOG OUT	68

CLUES

PREDICTION

After all the screaming, pushing, tearing,
the moment of elation as she emerges,
scarlet and squalling, while everyone else
kisses, embraces, then suddenly stiffens.
She is rushed away and the room holds its breath.
The consultant approaches, trying to pull his face
out of a grimace and into a kind of smile,
as he clasps your hand and says,
I'm sorry, but you have just given birth
to a poet.

Let me explain, he says.
She will not be like other people. Ever.
She will be the kind of child
that you encourage to be herself,
then bitterly regret it
when she does just that.

Is there any history of poetry in the family?
Ah. A grandfather who wrote limericks
and an aunt who dabbled in haiku.
Yes, this is a common mutation.
Let's pray it's not a severe strain,
and she's only occasionally subject
to wild fantasies and intermittent depression.

Rest assured, we'll do our utmost
to help you manage her creative predilections.
You'll need to keep her away
from fountain pens and notebooks.
Give her plenty of robust exercise
and above all, teach her the value
of a proper day's work,
for poets are an idle lot.

After all, it is unlikely that she will be any good.
You can steer her away from the poet's life
of debt, insanity and promiscuity

by encouraging her to take up
an admin role at a university or art gallery.
When she complains
about there being something missing,
suggest Prozac, even homeopathy.

After her divorce, her mid-life crisis
will involve slipping into a no-woman's land
of dreaming, scheming,
and a second career as a life coach,
or creative writing tutor,
where she will teach other poets to become
creative writing tutors.

Let her. It will act as an anaesthetic.
You see, this syndrome is incurable.
Whatever you do,
whatever treatment we prescribe,
she will keep trying to be a poet.

Remember, you didn't do anything wrong.
Do your best to love her anyway.
There's still a small chance that one day
she will cause you to be proud.

THE CASE AGAINST ACROBATICS

Who wants to go into all the acrobatics of the wedding night?
                    Violet Winspear, Mills & Boon novelist

When I was a child I thought
sex happened sideways.
That two people faced each other,
and like the cross-section
in a biology textbook,
their parts interwove perfectly.

Father once hinted that
it was a bit like parking –
all a question of geometry –
and Mummy alluded to hosepipes
and a rather happy daffodil.

I never realised they got
on top of each other.
Mounted. Serviced.
Knelt down, bent over.
Riding, bucking,
peaking, thrusting,
licking, sucking, blowing —

no one mentioned these.
Or the stink of sweat, gas,
the aniseed of raw meat,
the question of residue.

Still, I maintain my search
for limbs that tuck away neatly,
a hint of French parfum,
the smooth glide
of a pearl-handled butter knife.

I am after all, an idealist,
fond of a little light Mozart
and the gasp that follows
the opening of a small velvet box.

THERE WAS THIS GIRL AT THE CRICKET WHO

leapt onto the
pitch. Clothes
absent, hair
flying, arms
akimbo.
Air penetrating
everywhere.

She cartwheeled
towards the slack-
jawed bowler,
the applauding crowd.

Skin luminescent,
it seemed all the world
had joined her:
a film of flesh
tilting and twisting
between the statuesque
and neatly pressed whites.

A policeman, of course,
caught up with her.
An arm shot across
her breasts,
a hand cupped
her pubic hair.

Suddenly
she'd noticed
the stares
penetrating
everywhere.

CHRISTMAS DAY: A MIRACLE

Walking has never been your forte,
especially not the sort your family enjoys;
not the sport for a would-be princess
dressed in various shades of pink,
carrying the make-up kit
you call your laptop.
But, having just applied
blue eye-shadow to your brother's face,
you must have felt emancipated,
because when challenged
to run like the wind, you did.

On stumpy legs you tromped your way
to the bottom of the hill.
But your spotted boots didn't stop there,
and we, your family, could only stare
as you charged across the headland,
past other families, barking dogs,
the withered tree that looked like a witch.
As fast as we could walk, you ran faster,
far beyond our eyeline, our faltering hearts
relieved of their belief that you
would soon run out of steam.

True, when you finally stopped,
overtaken by the violent urge to pee,
your wails echoed with mournful clarity.
But Dad ran to the rescue,
slid off your sodden underwear
and, in a moment of genius,
shed his own battered fleece
and created trousers
by pushing your feet through the sleeves.

We gathered round you, revelling in tales
of your marathon, marvelling at how far you'd run,
but you, hoisted onto Daddy's shoulders,

became unusually silent.
As he carried you home, your tears dried,
and raising your head as if wearing a crown,

you surveyed the horizon,
sensing, perhaps for the first time,
the freedom to be anything you wanted.

LOVE AND SIMILIAR MISUNDERSTANDINGS

CONFESSION

How did we get here?
We walked as close as we could
without touching,
wearing darkest possible sunglasses.

We lay down at the Cliffs of Moher
and hung our eyes over the edge,
the water so mesmerising
I saw myself jump right in
and understood those ancient heroes who…

But I can't, you said,
let go of everything.
I have a marriage to re-contract.
And beneath us the sea
bubbled and swallowed up rocks.

It was the dancing
that did it.
Hands on hips
lips on forehead
skin sticking to skin

we are flung
and an airstream
holds us buoyant
like the gulls floating
between the Cliffs of Moher.

For when we fall
so completely

there is always
something left
to catch us.

MOST OF OUR HISTORY WE FORGET

We were the original scallywags:
scabby-kneed, scuffed elbows,
making camp beneath the copper beech.

You showed me the slimy trails
that snails laid. I made you daisy chains
and you'd wear them, occasionally.

We both grew boisterous curly hair
but yours was finer, blonde, a halo.
Mine required a fight with a stiff brush.

In term-time I'd run home,
hungry for letters. Father, you wrote,
banned you from ballet lessons,

but smiled audibly
the next overheated and gauzy summer
when he caught us holding hands,

winked when you stole Pimm's for a riverside picnic,
overlooked our giggling in the warm, prickly grass,
your covert kisses to the top of my head.

By autumn, you were paler.
Angular when it came to arguments;
braver with daisy chains.

I remained faithful to a photo
of us sat on a park bench
sharing strawberry ice cream.

Your letters became scarce. Whispers
of a long stay abroad. Your name
dropped from family conversations.

Years later,
you sent me a copy of Maurice,
to explain.

LOVE STORY

New Year's Day and the bed is garlic
with damp and stale cigarettes.
Waking and, for a moment,
despite the numb nose, ice-curled toes,
everything is okay.
Then cracked lips licked, tongue of dried grit,
slide back beneath the covers.
Stupid cow.

Midday in the street, and it's drizzling.
A geezer shouts, *Happy New Year, you bastards!*
You slope to the corner shop, to buy a paper,
biscuits, something. Closed, of course.
You go home, make coffee.
The milk carton wears a sour skin.

It's the sort of thing to tell your mum,
but she'd only say, *Ahhh… cheer up.*
Worse things happen at sea.
As you fall down, throw up,
face a washed-out olive green.

Pick up your phone because he's a friend
and friends don't wear their guilt like bruises.
They talk. It's good to talk, remember?
Only here's where talking got you,
talk, talk, talk and cheap beer.

So it's ringing and you pray,
please go to answerphone…

Oh sorry, did I wake you?
Great party, yeah.
Listen, that thing I said, can we forget it?
When I asked if you would be my boyfriend?
You don't remember that bit.
It's okay. You said no.
See you later?

Stupid cow.

AGAINST LOVE

Her varicose veins itch
as she shifts her thighs
across the bar stool,
while Bob informs
the other pub husbands,
yet again,
that during the Second World War
the standard payload bay of Lancasters
had to be altered to accommodate
the heavier bombs required
to destroy the Ruhr Dam.

She calls that third glass of red wine
self-care,
as Bob's next anecdote
ends in the tagline
everyone fell about laughing.

Like the night he was so pissed
he slipped off his stool
and the edge of the bar sliced
his chin open.
Everyone fell about laughing.

The wine stings the pit in her lip.
He only splits it occasionally.
His father hit him,
so he does the same,
and love forgives, doesn't it?
When she threatened to quit,
he said, *Go on. If you think
you can find another prick
thick enough to stick with you.*

They were eighteen
when he said I fancy you.
She'd quivered like the flames
in her gran's gas fire,
and if that wasn't love
she would make it do.

Before she knew it,
they were up the aisle.
Knickers yanked aside quicker
than she meant them to.

She purses her lips for another sip.
Whitney bleats out that the greatest love
is learning to love yourself.
She never understood that.
Surely it only counted
if someone else loved you.
And come Saturday
Bob would still buy a line or two
for them to snort together.
After all, it's what Whitney would do.

The door swings open,
the draught fumbles up her skirt,
a napkin flies up and out.
She knows all she has to do
is pick up her coat and follow it.
But like her mother,
and her mother's mother before that,
she orders another drink,
as something she mistook for love
glues her to the stool.

ALPHA BITCH

On our wedding day
the registrar handed me
the marriage licence,
as if she knew
something I didn't.

She was right.
My husband shows
no interest
in the whereabouts
of our marriage licence.
Nor does he know
where his passport is
(I have hidden it)
or that it's expired.

If he intends to flee
with her (another, not
the registrar), he will
have to satisfy himself
with the Lakes. Or Cornwall.
Somewhere easily
within my reach.

This marriage is mine.
I have the certificate
to prove it.
He thinks I don't notice
him cocking his leg
on other lampposts,
because he only does it
when I, *the bitch*,
am out of town.

Roaming into gardens,
rummaging
in neighbours' bins
will earn him a slap
and a night in the kennel,

while the actual dog
gets to rest his head
next to mine on the pillow.

The marriage licence
was handed to me
on our wedding day.
He'll be happy again
when he remembers
his place in the pack.

HISTORY

Why you stood out on the shelf
was a mystery. The point of the toe, perhaps,
the shiny snakeskin uppers, heels clicked to attention
amongst sober pumps, sensible lace-ups, the kind
a mother would buy in early September.

I'd only run in for shelter from a sky filled
with grey fists, a holiday on a compromised budget,
but soon we were walking together,
squeaking on parquet floors,
sliding on grass, slippery with spring.

A little polish, and you became burnished.
Muscular with experience. Toes turned up
like the pert noses of petulant film stars.

We played footsie under dinner tables,
danced in the kitchen at parties,
marched together through several winters.

I don't know who stopped caring first,
but one night I caught you
passed out on the doormat,

weather bleeding from your soles,
sides splayed as if still inhabited,
block heels now unfashionable.

A pity I can't say farewell by text
or email. Too much history
to put in a bin.

A shelf, then. In a corner of the house
I rarely visit, where memories blur,
and I can pretend this chapter has an end.

IN THE STYLE OF JOHN OSBORNE

John Osborne only has one jumper,
the colour and texture of day-old porridge,
a fisherman's hessian sack that he wears
to gigs, in London, for photoshoots.

One day, my husband met John in the street.
The jumper hugged him like an old friend.
John had come from a press junket –
his PR person wore a suit – but John must have felt
his jumper was sufficient. As he said,
It was only for Channel Five.

John Osborne only has one jumper
and when he performs his poetry
he twists his hands up into his sleeves,
as if he were still at primary school,
as if his hands wished to disappear.
The jumper hangs low over his hips,
though not long enough to prevent
John revealing his butt cheeks
when he squats down to pick up a pint,
carefully left at the foot of the mic.

John Osborne only has one jumper
but my sister has forty-three pairs of jeans.
Her husband counted them one morning
while she made breakfast for the kids.
Actually, he counted thirty-seven, but she admitted
she had one pair on, three on the line
and two in the wash-basket. She told him
because honesty is important in a marriage.

I only have four pairs of trousers.
Like John, I have learnt that everything I need
can be fitted into one suitcase, or borrowed.
After all, there are always saucepans
and ironing boards standing idle.
Libraries filled with books aching to be read.

John Osborne only has one jumper
and his loyalty to it makes me think
that whomever he marries will be deeply loved.
John will not mind if they get saggy
or start to gape.
He will still wear them with pride.

ON MARRIAGE

It's morning, so I go to the kitchen
and find you have left me
dirty wine glasses filled
with smashed pistachio shells.
I put the milk back in the fridge
and rinse out Tupperware, greasy
with congealing curry sauce.

I call these things love tokens,
symbols of your devotion,
and I call them that
because cursing you
when you leave last night's
late-night snack everywhere
hurts me, not you.

On the landing stands
a stack of bank statements,
credit card offers, wage slips
and bills that you claim,
and have claimed, for some time,
you will deal with… soon.
The top sheets are sun-bleached
and dust puffs off them as I brush past.

More love tokens,
symbols of your devotion,
and I call them that
because cursing you
when you leave
your shit everywhere
hurts me, not you.

Next I visit the bathroom.
There are damp socks in the sink
and dark matter clinging
to the porcelain,
which I know you'll say
will wash away by itself
if we flush enough times.

Even more love tokens,
symbols of your devotion,
and I call them that
because cursing you
when you leave
your actual shit everywhere
hurts me, not you.

I could say these things mean
you don't care.
Present them as evidence
that you don't meet
the standards agreed
by normal people.

But instead I call them
love tokens.
Because cursing you
when you don't behave
the way I want you to
hurts me, not you,
bruises me, not you,
punishes me, not you.

Besides, I made a promise
to love all of you.
And, true, I didn't know
exactly what that entailed,
but at least I'm learning
what not to do.

Like cursing you
for simply being you.

RELUCTANT FEMINIST

WALKING TO WORK

after Neruda

It so happens I am sick of being a woman.
And it happens that I walk past windows filled with mannequins,
clothes hanging off them like discarded intestines.
I hate their gaping mouths, opaque eyes, sunken cheeks,

while around me, their limping facsimiles
teeter on splinters, hormones boiled into their faces,
faith erased from intimate places.
Still, wouldn't it be wonderful to cut out their voiceboxes,
silence the vox pops, and never sew them back?

It so happens I am sick of being a woman;
glancing off tourists with Mormon haircuts,
college eyebrows, knee-high white socks,
drifting in swarms between Burger King and Starbucks,

trudging past hoardings that parade false prophecies
to crossroads, where torsos hunch over steering wheels
inside furious metal cats that snap at each other's tails.

Down, down past the houses herded into streets,
crammed into stalls, while beneath, the rats,
oblivious to doors, locks, fences, make their own highways,
don't bother with polite conversation about the weather,
but gnaw through any fibre or wire that gets in their way.

It so happens I am sick of my hands, my hips, my feet;
yet when Monday flares up, with her line of corpses at bus stops,
chewed up, bombed out, salt-sick,
I bow my head and, howlingly serene,
open the door to a fume-scalded building,
ignoring Monday's disguise;
an old woman walking by,
a single hair curling out of her head,
which I could grab,

but I don't.

REDRESS

after Kim Addonizio

I want a red dress.
One that fits like a flame,
licking my frame so sleekly
it says, You can't stop this, bro.
I want to slink past all those Rolexes
and for them to know
they are shackled in my presence.
I want this red dress to be a blessing,
I want it to be a skin to me,
stretch with me,
I want that dress to cup my breasts
like the precious flesh they've always been.

Except for the first two days of my period,
when the material should soften
and ruffle round my engorged middle.
Or if someone dies. Then I'll formalise
and grow sleeves.
But not for job interviews, PTAs
or speeches to the UN.

That red dress has always hung
in our closet. But we forget to wear it,
distracted by the minutiae
of playing grey.

We're already cooking, cleaning,
having the babies, running companies,
oh, and the country,
but if we put on our red dresses

what could we do then?
What could we actually do?

DREAM DATE

Donald Trump asked me to the cinema last night.
He'd had a hard day on the campaign trail
and wanted someone to unwind with.

It was a dream, of course,
but vivid enough to stay alive
deep into the day.

Donald Trump, even dream Donald,
is troubled, broken, orange.
A snapped-off piece of my psyche
reminding me that I have not always
been fond of women.

In my time I've sneered at martyrs,
manipulators, dumb blondes,
victims, gold diggers, crybabies, frauds.
Barbie dolls, plastic surgery addicts,
Lycra-sealed aerobics instructors, earth mothers,
health-at-any-sizers. Pluckers, liposuckers,
boob enhancers, wrinkle deniers. Yoginis,
bikini body-seekers and those partial
to the actor's dose of Botox.

I've despised these masks.
And worn all of them.

There are days I pretend misogyny
doesn't exist anymore.
Truth is, I'm bored
of having to point it out
time and again.

Especially the little things.
*Daft mare, silly cow,
calm down, dear,
we're only having a laugh.*

A pudgy, orange hand reaches out.
Do I dare put an arm around my inner Donald,
give its shoulders a squeeze, and say,
You're such an angry syrup.
You Tango-faced slanderer of women?

And if I do embrace it,
might the real Donald Trump
wake up one morning, bewildered,
hair rumpled, yet still cosy,
mumbling a poem in praise of Hillary?

THE BECHDEL TEST

Oh look, my mother says. *Tits.*
We're in the Ashmolean
and having wandered past
an eight-foot stone god
holding his phallus –
which made both of us roll our eyes,
and mouth, *Typical* –
perhaps she feels an urge for balance,
as a hand-sized clay goddess
catches her eye.

Tits. Not a word
my mother often uses.
She sniffs and wriggles
her shoulders. *I am a Lloyd*,
she says, and yes, *tits*
are exactly what my grandfather
would have pointed out.

We haven't been on a jaunt
for a while. Left by himself,
my father's thoughts twist
into fibrous knots.
He would prefer them purged,
sorted into files, laid to rest.
As he constantly attempts
with each rearrangement
of the garage.

Today we try to discuss other things.
The X-ray of a mummified child king.
Master ceramicists responsible
for intricate blue and white,
the superiority of Earl Grey
over builders' tea.

When we get home, Father shouts,
Stand up straight! You look
like an old woman. Don't giggle

about your varicose veins.
They're serious.

We must do this again,
my mother says
as we kiss goodbye.
I'm glad she's gone deaf
in one ear, and drinks
a half-bottle of Prosecco
on alternate nights.

Though when I call to say thank you,
Prosecco has been banned.
He's decided it's bad for her health.

LETTER TO MY HEADMISTRESS

Miss Dunn, that day in RE class you said
the man you stood behind in the shop,
who kept effing this and effing that, was lazy.
That swearing betrayed a lack of imagination
and we should strive to find more potent words.
My eleven-year-old self was also displeasured
by such riffraff, so vowed, in future,
to describe Jane, for instance,
as extremely, wondrously,
ambidextrously gorgeous.

But you know what, Miss Dunn?
Extremely, wondrously, even *ambidextrously*
will never convey the majesty of
Jane is fucking gorgeous.
Fuck is such a lovely word.
So flexible, so passionate, so many uses.
Peter fucks Jane.
Jane is fucked by Peter.
Oh fuck. Jane is fucking pregnant.

Miss Dunn, I've realised you're not a woman
who knew the value of a good fuck.
But you're not alone.
In America, or, more precisely,
Battlestar Galactica,
they say *frack.*
Meddling with a couple of letters placated
the censors, and those sensibilities roughened
by the guttural earthiness of it all.
But when Commander Adama says,
Let's get the frack out of here,
it's clear what he means.

Because sometimes, Miss Dunn,
you just have to say it.
I know you wished us a life
of Cath Kidston tablecloths
and Emma Bridgewater mugs.

Believed the love of Jesus
and being polite would help
us avoid the darkness.
But it's not enough, Miss Dunn.

Because fuck is a cry of freedom.
As it blasts out of our mouths,
it takes with it all the bitterness,
anguish and tears which, if swallowed
back down, macerate our guts.
In other words, Miss Dunn, we get fracked.
That's what happens when you apply
intolerably high pressure to vital organs.

Miss Dunn, that day in RE class you preached
abstinence from unladylike words,
whilst your dog Dougal humped
my leg. You growled,
and for a moment it worked,
but his half-hearted air thrusts
showed what was still on his mind.

Miss Dunn, you never married.
For you, an out-of-wedlock shag
would have been out of the question,
but I do hope that one time, your lips
curled around this wonderful word,
and you got to savour the juice-inducing
flavour of a good fuck.

THE SLIP

CONSIDER THE CUPCAKE

Consider its curves,
its whips, its whirls,
consider the glint
of its frosting.
The way it tickles
your fancy, whispering,
Lick me.

Consider you promised
not to eat them again,
but the ache in your gut
insists you're hungry
for something.
And it's just
an ickle cupcake,
whispering,
Lick me, lick me.

And the hollow grows
with every glance,
your conscience and desire
in an intricate dance,
because you're hungry
for something,
and the more you say *No*,
the more you want to;
the more you say *Don't*,
the more it shouts *Do*!
*You're hungry
for something,
for God's sake,
lick me, lick me, lick me.*

So strip off the casing,
heart racing at each rip.
Dip your finger in the icing,
let your teeth penetrate.
Close your eyes,
dream of parties

back when life was fun,
as its sweetness disperses
on your impatient tongue.

So you've licked.
Deed done.
Your stomach seems full,
but your mind screams, More!
And as you've broken
your promise anyway…

Stick another in your mouth
even faster than the last.
No time to feel queasy,
no chance to grasp
that you're starving
for something
much larger than cake.
Plugging the gap
with carbohydrates,
seduced by the wiles
of sugar and glaze,
caught in a spiral

you thought was escape.

REASONS TO BE GOOD

Reason 1. God will love me

God is CCTV.
Sees every sweet I pinch,
every lie I lip synch,
stores those recordings
and takes note of the score.
So I keep all ten commandments,
even the ones that don't make sense,
because the world is an ark,
the rules are my guard rail,
and I'm not the sort who can get away
with walking on water.

Reason 2. My parents will love me

I sprang into this world as a cherub
who could do no wrong,
but before long discovered
a list of demands
that must be met
to guarantee the peace.
So I pull my socks up,
tie my hair back,
finish that homework.
Obey commands like,
Because I told you so,
because my father
told me so.
Do my best to believe
everything's fine,
even as they wipe the tears
from my eyes.

Reason 3. Other people will like me

If you ask me a favour, I'll say yes.
Even if yes tastes rotten.
Even as I work out

what yes will cost me,
because saying yes means I'm nice.
And I need to know I'm nice,
because deep down I'm convinced
I'm an arsehole.
But I need to hit the right level:
above mediocre, below eye-catching.
After all, no one likes a smart-arse… hole.

Reason 4. Be good because it's simpler

I mustn't be the grit that sticks
in other people's noses.
Mucus makes life so clingy.
So I go with the flow,
don't rock the boat,
keep it clean, ordered, smooth,
a bit like Sweden.
If I have to speak,
I choose words sugary enough
for a Mother's Day card,
and if I must write a poem,
I make sure it's the sort that rhymes.

Reason 5. I'll get the prize

So I've ticked the boxes,
filled out forms,
submitted card details,
maybe now I can breathe.
Maybe now the jittering bees
in my head will sleep awhile,
my mouth taste of honey again.
Just as long as I stay on track
for leader of the pack,
top of the class, best in show,
crème de la crème,
I'll live happily ever after,

no matter the cost right now.

CARCASSONNE

In this life
we will grow lemons,
make onion soup
and cassoulet from scratch.

Buy from market stalls
stuffed with bundles of fresh herbs,
loaves piled like driftwood,
walnuts, olives, apricots.

Accept the rabbits
locked in rusty cages
unknowingly contemplating
their final hours.

Drink minute coffees
at extreme leisure.
Eat croissants without
suffering gluten intolerance.

Still, the wind will howl,
the rain pummel us,
as in our other life,
but it won't be important.
Instead they will carve
new stories into our faces,

whisper that we can only own
places with our eyes,
and the steep castle walls
will define where we stand
in the grand history of things.

LOST THINGS

To remember or to forget – which is healthier?

Anna Funder, *Stasiland*

Sometimes it occurs when moving,
you come across some foreign coins
sleeping in a drawer you had
no useful reason to open again.

Yet here you are,
standing at a forgotten peepshow,
ready to slide these tokens
into the slot.

Perhaps you sense the surge of mountain ranges,
border crossings, previous friendships.
The flies, trinket shops, fellow travellers.
The earth's stone masonry indifferent to your presence.

There is always what happened
and what really happened.

So sweep them into a plastic bag,
deposit in a pot for unwanted holiday change
at some bank, some charity shop,

leave, swaddled in pride,
breathing easier,
a whiff of metal still
on your fingers.

COLD CALL

So, man with a heavy Delhi accent,
claiming to be called Sebastian,
you want to know how I am today.
Fine, *thanks* and *Yes,*
I'll take part in your survey.

What I don't say is, I'm twitchy.
I've got that low-grade itch,
the fidgety heartbeat,
and even as I choose
a mark out of ten
for how interested
I am in the RNIB,
there's a starting pistol
firing inside me.

Frankly, Sebastian, I'm a mess.
Do you ever feel your life is meaningless?
Ken in the pub says we're here to procreate,
and that's it. Life destined to beget life.
But I believe there's more,
like an honest answer to the question,
how are you today?

What age bracket am I in?
46–54, since you're asking.
Yes, I am more likely to give money
to dog rescue than cancer prevention.
Does that make me some sort of animal?

Listen, Sebastian, I'm still trying
to answer your first question.
But I'm distracted,
and call it sixth sense,
call it a woman's intuition,
but something tells me
you are not called Sebastian.

I don't blame you for agreeing to use
an alias that appeals to my Britishness.
This script you've memorised
isn't yours, and I ache
at the dissonance you must feel every day
as you float away from your true name.

Are you on Facebook, Sebastian?
Because I'm scanning
my other phone,
and, according to this meme,
fear is nothing to be afraid of.
Isn't that amazing, Sebastian?
Could it be the answer to everything?

How am I today?
Fear is nothing to be afraid of.
What age bracket am I?
Nothing to be afraid of.
Going blind or contracting cancer?
Nothing to be afraid of.

Sebastian.
What are you afraid of?
Sebastian?

DRONE

The poet, it turned out, was less useful
than we'd been led to believe.
Oh, that breathing back into our bones
was soothing, and the nuggets of crystallised wisdom,
sublime. A day spent groping for words
instead of tapping numbers into spreadsheets,
well, you could pay me for that any time.

But she hung around, like a cassette at a digital conference.
Stonewashed jeans rising above striped socks,
head slipped around doors, whispering,
Here's a sonnet about loss,
the moment you shook hands on a deal.

All because British Airways made a profit
after a poet wrote a piece called 'Working Together'.
Somebody up high thought poetry
would be good for morale,
help us find meaning in our work.
Distract us, more likely, and if we'd known
what we were being distracted from,
we might have paid more attention.

The computers moved in, you see.
Turns out they don't need pee breaks
or maternity leave. Don't need
to stare at stars to feel human again,
and as much as customers despise
talking to automated voices, they soon forget
if offered cheap home insurance.

I wish I hadn't run away from the poet.
I wish I'd had a window and looked at the sky more.
I might've seen what the wind was blowing in.
How we too were the telephone with a rotary dial,
the box-shaped TV, the manual typewriter,
which would work
if only you could find
the right sort of ribbon.

FAILURE, YOU MAKE ME INTERESTING

Give me stories to tell at dinner parties
where others market themselves as heroes.
The corporate veneers fell off my teeth years ago;
I couldn't maintain that winning smile,
that homogenised glow,
so let's forget your bland doppelgänger, success,
and let me praise you for all the lows.

Thank you for the film stars
who didn't send roses or pink limousines,
and their facsimiles in the wine bars
of my youth who, with a single glance,
bestowed upon me the superpower of invisibility.
As I was also a facsimile of myself back then,
let me cherish those lucky escapes
and praise you, like I should.

Thanks too for my love affair with an art form
that is the world's worst career move,
with more exponents than Justin Bieber's
got Beliebers, and less audience
than an arachnid's fan club.
I mean they do exist, but mainly
in the corners of condemned buildings.
Still, poets make generous friends
(until someone gets a book deal).
Even then, let me praise you, like I should.

Failure, we've come a long way together.
You've gifted me with pouchy cheeks,
cellulite drawers. You're the midnight bar
of Cadbury's, when the diet's
run short of aphorisms.
Thank you for all the jobs I didn't get,
the medals I didn't win,
the orgasms I didn't have,
and all the ones I faked.

If I'd won those battles,
I'd be constantly on the run,
chanting, *Failure is not an option*,
when you absolutely are,
so let me celebrate you, failure.
Let me praise you, like I should.

BROUGHT TO MY KNEES

BECAUSE I LOVE ANIMALS, DON'T I

Every morning I am woken by the ducks
laughing their throaty comments
as they run drunkenly from the stable,
jostling, stumbling into puddles,
their beaks curved into a smile,
and on Christmas Day, I shall eat one of them.

Isabel, latter-day Buddhist, tells me
if I won't take a knife to their throats myself,
I have no right to make one my lunch.
She sends me a recipe for nut roast
and a glutinous, hot tar drips down my back.

When I was a child, they used to say,
Where you have livestock, there'll be dead stock,
but there was always a man
or a disease around to do the killing.

Like Flynn. Whose snapped leg swung
as his lips screamed back,
body rigid with shivers,
until the bolt hit his star
and the shuddering stopped,
and the earth was pounded by an empty horse.

NOBODY SAID

Urine, viscous as cooking oil,
sludges from catheter to bag.
His legs, an A-frame more spindly
than the tent poles he used to curse
as he struggled to construct
a holiday out of canvas.
All Vesta curries, chip shops closed at five
and the drip of Ilfracombe rain,
so your mum could play Wendy House
and you could do… *whatever kids did.*

A word is draped over every bed.
Held at bay by antiseptic green uniforms
and ticks on clipboards.
No one looks at the word, or whispers
the questions they need to ask.
To do so might jinx the miracle fixed
in your mum's arthritic grip.

He slipped through the morphine fog at 3am.
Driving with the headlights off,
guess he didn't see the cliff edge.
Left a crossword with few clues filled in.
Only expressed a preference
for things he didn't like:
God, *EastEnders*, people who laugh
too loud in restaurants.

We settle for Hank Marvin
to accompany his departure.
It may have been what he wanted.

We don't know.

NOT YET

i.m. Chris Geoghegan, 1969–2013

The news we knew would come
arrived via Facebook.
Passed away peacefully
after a brave fight.
His last words: Not yet.

Not yet.
Was he merely insisting
that the massage therapist,
standing next to his bed,
wait a moment?

Not yet.
That his nappy
didn't need changing?

Not yet.
Despite the screams
that punctuated his sedation.

Not yet
ready to leave behind
dreams of steam trains,
a decent sex life,
Far East adventures.

Not yet
packed to leave.
Flight information
hazy but inevitable.
An outbound breath
that never returned.

EVACUATION

This is the room of everyday
tragedies. It is ice-silent,
silent as children are not.

Thoughtfully, someone has stuck
a poster on the door: a woman stroking
her smooth, domed belly.

Everyone stares elsewhere.
The wall, the sheets,
the fog-bitten snow.

We are bandaged, sedated,
made naked under white gowns,
even wedding rings removed.

Leave the remainder
of a year's dreams
in a bucket.

Return home raw,
ordinary again.

FUTURE PLANS

I will be a woman who borrows
other women's stories about children.
I will only have myself to blame
for nights without sleep.

I will sit quietly on a girls' night out,
contemplating my freedoms and losses;
no bullying, failed exams or lost shoes
for me to handle.

I will be a member of a group
of marvellous women, who happen
not to have babies. Who are
the end of the line.

Still, the world carries on.
It weaves around me, vibrant
with a thousand more urgent
worries than this:

a thread left hanging loose
when the great tapestry was sewn.

SIREN

And isn't it sometimes
that you stand on a shore
and the constant pulse
beckons to you over and over?

The waves want to draw you under,
to know you as water again,
and doesn't it always feel right,
surging with the certainty of lust?

Your own rivers sing back,
plunge towards this future-echo
calling you to free yourself of flesh
with all its limps and bruises.

They forget they once desired a body,
an imagination to call their own.
So the body must say, *Yes, yes, one day,*
but there's still work on land to be done.

TODAY

TWO DRESSES

Hot lights in the changing-room cubicle.
Two dresses, one red, one green.
Both times I emerge,
the assistant oohs and aahs.
She's cast herself as the friend
I should have brought with me.
You know your curves
are the perfect curves for these styles.
I arch an eyebrow, but I suspect she's right.
You know, you should buy both.
I shrug.
My bank balance would disagree.
She sweeps her hair back.
Personally, I'd rather eat less
than miss out on something beautiful.

I nod, and smile.
Like this is a rational argument.
I'm not being rude
but I doubt she's ever made
the choice between a dress and food.
I want to talk about
the benefits of decent nutrition
but she's turned to her friend.
I fancy a coffee. Lend me a fiver?

I retire to the changing room.
Make sure you listen to the voice
that says go for it!
I flinch, cinch
my shoulders up to my ears,
because I can hear
myself considering it.

I prefer the green, I say.

The red is the last in the shop.

My gut twists.
Suddenly I imagine
there's a dress famine,
and I will never find another
that fits me this well.

You could give up cake.

My hands shake
as I hold the two dresses up.
Red or green. Red or green.
Red and green?

I caress the wrinkled edges
of the notes in my purse.
Fingers creep towards plastic.
The newly sober reaching
for a first sip.

You do have a credit card, don't you?

Hand snaps back.
Hangs the red dress up.

The corners of her mouth curl down.
You listened to the wrong voice.
You'll be back in ten minutes.
I nod and smile. Think, thank God,
my parking ticket runs out in ten minutes.
Then I'll drive home and have dinner
in a dress that's completely mine.

After all, I can only ever wear
one dress at a time.

I WILL NOT MAKE GREAT ART TODAY

Because a cobweb, crocheted across a high corner,
quivers seductively at me, and no doubt
once I have sucked it out of existence,
errant ladybirds, dog hair and biscuit crumbs
will breeze forth, cause me to grip
the hoover with the fervour of an addict
muttering, Just one more hit.

I will not make great art today,
because I can't stop thinking about a story
Leslie Long told me last night,
of arriving home after an interminable day at the office
and the obligatory evil of exchange at her local Asda,
finally able to drop her shopping bags
and let out a whipcrack of a fart,
only to turn round and see her husband sitting there
with the local planning officer.
Apparently no one knew what to say,
but they did get permission for a large extension.

I will not make a great art today
because I don't understand why,
at the age of forty-eight, I still find farting
so funny. Nor can I sneak in
a reference to Descartes,
though it sort of rhymes,
or how the smell might evoke
a Proustian response,
or a philosophical musing
on whether an unobserved fart
still makes a sound…

I will not make great art today
because I don't know how great art starts.
But I sense great art should know
it's great art, and behave accordingly.
I will not make a great art today
because I am not a great artist,
but a jobbing poet who jogs along

at the back of the pack, dressed
in a faded velour tracksuit.

So today, I will make small art.
Sketch out a one-inch square of detail.
Sobering though it is,
if the great artist stomps off elsewhere
to compose the most eloquent epigrams,
pantoums and sestinas ever written,
this small artist may quieten enough
to hear how the blackbird sings.

And thus she might become a great artist.
But not until two hundred years after her death,
when a student, clearing out
her great-grandmother's house, discovers,
amongst the moth-eaten tinsel
and dusty diamanté jewellery,
a poetry pamphlet, whose edges
have been nibbled by mice.

And if she begins to read,
maybe, just maybe,
after turning a couple of pages,
she'll settle down to read a couple more.

THERE'S NO MONEY IN POETRY, BUT THEN THERE'S NO POETRY IN MONEY EITHER

title from Robert Graves

Mr Graves, I disagree.
Extraordinary poet that you were,
I believe you fell in love
with the joyful symmetry
of that sentence,
much as one might luxuriate
in the harmony and balance
of Georgian architecture.

But imagine, Mr Graves,
if we treated money
like poetry. Explored
it as a metaphor, played
with its form, wrestled
with the language
until we uncovered
a greater truth.

If we call money *filthy lucre*,
pinch our noses at its rotten stink,
call it the root of all evil,
are we not abusing it?
For wonga, dosh, bread, moolah,
smackers were our creation.
Money is as innocent as a puppy, Mr Graves;
if it turns into a snarling beast,
it is the owners who made it so.

Mr Graves, let me be clear.
Sometimes, money is more elusive
than the final rhyme of a sonnet,
seems to tease like the muse
beckoning you to the desk,
only to stick two fingers up at you.

But doesn't that always happen
when you grasp for an image
as if your life depended on it?

And whilst I agree we're not about
to float poetry on the Stock Exchange,
penurious as you were, Mr Graves,
would you rather have been anything
other than a poet?
Even when fighting for your life
in the bloodied swamps
of the Somme,
you found poetry in them.
Why would the trenches
of money be any different?

Of course, when I say
treat money like poetry,
there is the other way.
Ignore it, deride it,
think it's only for the elite.
Need I go on, Mr Graves?
Suffice to say,
we have regarded poetry
as disdainfully
as we've regarded money.

But being a poet has made me rich, Mr Graves.
I can cry in equal measure at a sunrise
or a deathbed.
Let's not waste a fine metaphor.
Because, earn, spend, save or give it away,
I can make money a numb transaction,
or if I choose, there can be poetry
in the exchange.

LET YOUR DOG OUT

Please. Don't be good.
Forget what parents, teachers,
lovers say. Wear stripes
with spots, trot to the shops
in a dressing gown, if it tickles you.

Please don't be good.
There's so little space
between *g* and *d*,
two circles to shackle
your feet, while you type
tomorrow's essay,
report, obituary.

Please, be a dog.
Play like a dog,
work like a dog,
love like a dog,
tail wagging,
paws scrabbling,
until, tongue lolling,
you corpse out in the sun,
refusing to move,
unless someone throws a stick
you can't resist.

Oh please, be a dog.
Rejoice in limbs,
spin until giddy.
Greet friends as travellers
returned from the high seas,
even when they've only been gone
five minutes,
and while you might not
sniff someone's arse
when you meet them,
consider trusting your nose
over what's written
on their CV.

Have undying faith
in the healing properties of sleep.
And if you want five pillows
to curl up on, or lie on your back,
hind legs curved in Celtic prayer,
airing your genitals, then do it.

Come on. Let your dog out.
Let it sniff about,
find the trail
that's most enticing;
if you don't,
it'll keep whining anyway.
So toilet train it,
but don't over-domesticate it
or smack it across the nose
with a manual
on how to behave.

But play like a dog,
work like a dog,
love like a dog,
tail wagging,
paws scrabbling,
until, tongue lolling,
you corpse out in the sun.

ACKNOWLEDGEMENTS

They say it takes a village to raise a child. For me, it was more like a county. So to the many people who helped with the creation of this book, thank you.

And in particular, Alan Buckley, Dan Holloway, David Olsen, Paul Surman and Paula Varjack for incisive and timely feedback.

Lucy Ayrton and Steve Larkin, for many years of support and encouragement.
Rachel Mae Brady, for being an inspirational director.

PBH's Edinburgh Free Fringe, Hammer & Tongue and countless gigs, festivals and poetry nights for the many chances to hone my craft as a performer.

All the occupants of Rowdy-ville, extraordinary women without whose guidance, love and support I would not have been half as daring as I am.

Neil Spokes, who has suffered more for my art than he could possibly have imagined when he signed the marriage certificate.